Café au Lait

Paper Piece a Rocky Road to Kansas

By Edie McGinnis

Editor: **Deb Rowden**
Designer: **Kim Walsh**
Photography: **Aaron T. Leimkuehler**
Illustration: **Eric Sears**
Technical Editor: **Jane Miller**
Production assistance: **Jo Ann Groves**

Published by:
Kansas City Star Books
1729 Grand Blvd.
Kansas City, Missouri, USA 64108

First edition, first printing
ISBN: 978-1-935362-63-0

Printed in the United States of
America by Walsworth Publishing Co.,
Marceline, MO

To order copies, call StarInfo at
(816) 234-4636 and say "Books."

PickleDish.com
The Quilter's Home Page

www.PickleDish.com

Contents

Introduction

Color choice . . . it's everything in a quilt. It's the light that shines, the shadow that's cast, and the place for one's eye to rest. It can bring a quilt to life or kill it.

We all have our favorite color, mine happens to be red. Not the bright fire-engine red but the red that has a bit of a blue cast to it or the red that reminds us of bricks. I love the spark that a bit of red gives to a quilt.

By the same token, we all have colors that are a challenge to work with. My biggest stumbling blocks have been browns and taupes. I understand why I have never liked those colors. When I wear clothing that is taupe or tan, all of the color washes out of my face. I suddenly look like I died and someone forgot to shovel dirt on me.

There does come a time to put away our aversions if we want to grow as quilters. When we decide there are "bad" colors and "good" colors, we shortchange ourselves and all our quilts begin to look alike. If we always gravitate toward the same colors, a folded stack of quilts takes on a haunting sameness.

My leap outside my particular color box occurred one year at Quilt Market during Sample Spree (a special session when vendors can shop). I bought a whole line of fabric from Daiwabo (a Japanese fabric company) in the form of fat eighths. The fabric collection was called "The Taupe Collection", designed by Junko Matsuda.

In the packets were plaids - not wild or bright like the Scot's Tartans, but soft, subtle shades woven through the backgrounds. The look of the fabric changed when the light shifted.

Some pieces had a wool slub woven in. I kept running my fingers over them, feeling the nubby texture and was reminded of pussy willow catkins. The fabric was such a change from the smooth cottons I've always used for quilting.

I couldn't wait to show my fabric find to my quilting friends. Their reactions were pretty amusing and ranged from, "That sure doesn't look like you!" to "I can't believe you bought that!"

I put my packets of fabric away and the next time I went to market I bought the new line of The Taupe Collection in the fat eighth bundles. Each market I went to Sample Spree, I looked for the Daiwabo booth and bought my fat eighths.

The packets were piling up in my sewing room and I had yet to figure out what I would make. I don't mind letting my fabric age a bit until the right idea comes along. If I wasn't careful though, that fabric was going to be like fine wine.

I came across a photo one day that showed a portion of an old Rocky Road to Kansas quilt. It looked like it had been made from grey and black wool and tied using red yarn. I thought about my packets of fabric, went to my computer and started playing around with the pattern.

I shifted some lines in the pattern, redrew others, added lines and took some away in the four legs of the star and turned it into a paper piecing pattern. I laid it out in rows and started to play with the backgrounds. It just seemed too boring when I used the same background color again and again.

It wasn't long before I was cutting up my fat eighths with abandon. Yarn dyes, plaids, stripes – they all went into the quilt. (That's the beauty of paper piecing!)

Wait! What in the world was I doing! I was deliberately making a brown and taupe quilt! Had I lost my mind or had I simply grown as a quilter? I'll let you be the judge.

Café au Lait ✣ **by Edie McGinnis** ✣ Paper Piece a Rocky Road to Kansas

Café au Lait
By Edie McGinnis

Quilted by Lori Kukuk

Quilt size: 70" x 85"

Block size: 15" finished

Fabric Requirements

❖ 25 assorted light fat eighths – each fat eighth yields 4 triangles or 2 pieces for position 8 and 2 pieces for position 9 on units A and B (see pages 14 and 15).

❖ 16 assorted medium brown fat eighths - each fat eighth yields 4 triangles or 2 pieces for position 8 and 2 pieces for position 9 (on units A and B).

❖ 42 assorted fat eighths of dark to medium dark browns or assorted fabrics to total 5 1/4 yards

❖ 1 1/4 yard medium brown for border

❖ 1 light fat eighth for border corner pieces

❖ 3/4 yard dark brown for binding

Supply List

❖ Add-A-Quarter ruler

❖ Rotary cutter and mat

❖ Template plastic or a note card

❖ Foundation paper - I recommend using Carol Doak's Foundation Paper. You need to make 20 - 15" blocks. Each block uses 2 - A units and 2 - B units so make 40 copies of each unit.

❖ Double-sided sticky tape

Cutting Directions

For positions 8 and 9 for both Unit A and Unit B

From light fat eighths, cut
50 – 6" x 10" rectangles
Place one rectangle atop another with right sides facing. Cut once from corner to corner on the diagonal. Reserve 4 triangles for the border.

From medium fat eighths, cut
32 – 6" x 10" rectangles
Place one rectangle atop another with right sides facing. Cut once from corner to corner on the diagonal.

Note: The objective is to have reverse pieces for positions 8 and 9 on both units. The easiest way to accomplish this is to make sure your fabric is folded with right sides facing before making any cuts.

From the dark brown and medium dark brown fat eighths, cut the following pieces. Mix up the fabrics and sew them into different positions to add interest and contrast to the blocks. Don't hesitate to layer the fabrics to speed up the cutting process.

Unit A – position 3 and Unit B – position 1 – Cut 40 – 5" squares. Cut the squares once on the diagonal making 80 triangles.

Unit A – position 1	40 – 5 1/4" x 3 1/2" rectangles
Unit A – position 2	40 – 6" x 3" rectangles
Unit A – position 4	40 – 4 1/2" x 3" rectangles
Unit A – position 5	40 – 3 1/2" x 2 1/4" rectangles
Unit A – position 6	40 – 2 1/2" x 2 1/4" rectangles
Unit A – position 7	40 – 1 3/4" x 2 1/2" rectangles

Unit B – position 2	40 – 6 1/4" x 2 1/2" rectangles
Unit B – position 3	40 – 5 3/4" x 3" rectangles
Unit B – position 4	40 – 4 3/4" x 2 3/4" rectangles
Unit B – position 5	40 – 3 3/4" x 3" rectangles
Unit B – position 6	40 – 2 3/4" x 2" rectangles
Unit B – position 7	40 – 1 3/4" x 2 1/2" rectangles

Border
From a light fabric, cut 4 – 5 1/2" squares
From a medium fabric, cut 8 – 5 1/2" strips across the width of the fabric.

Piecing the Units

Set up your sewing machine before you begin. Use a 90/14 needle and an open-toe presser foot. Set the stitch length to 18 – 20 stitches per inch. On my machine (a Bernina) that's 1.5.

Place a small piece of double-sided sticky tape on the blank side of the paper in position 1. The tape will adhere to the paper rather than the fabric. Put your first piece of fabric, right side up, in place. Put a piece of template plastic or a note card on the line, fold the paper back over the line. Place the Add-A-Quarter ruler up against the paper and trim between position 1 and 2.

Line up the edge of the fabric for position 2 with the first piece of fabric with right sides facing. Turn the paper over and stitch on the line between position 1 and position 2. Make sure you sew past the end of each line. Press each piece after it is sewn in place.

Fold the paper back on the line between position 2 and position 3. Butt the Add-A-Quarter ruler up to the paper and trim.

Continue on in this manner until you have all the dark brown pieces sewn to the paper. The final 2 pieces (8 and 9) will be added after you determine the unit's position in the quilt. Pin each unit to a design wall. If you don't have a design wall, lay them all out on a table so you have a clear view of the blocks.

Completing the Units

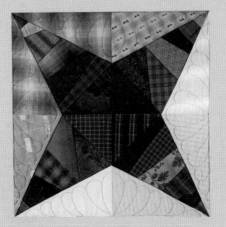

1.

Make 4 blocks using medium fabric around all 4 legs of the star (position 8 and position 9).

2.

Make 8 blocks using light fabric around both sides of I leg of the star, medium fabric around both sides of one leg of the star and 1 medium and 1 light around 2 legs of the star.

3.

Make 8 blocks using light fabric on all 4 legs of the star.

Trim each of the units before sewing them together. To do so, place the 1/4" line of a rotary cutting ruler on the outside solid line of the pattern. Then trim using your rotary cutter.

Before sewing the 4 sections of the block together, pin at each seam juncture. Baste only where the seams need to meet, using a large stitch on your machine. (Three stitches should do it.) Open and check to make sure the seams are matching, then sew the blocks together using a short stitch. Press as you sew.

Quilt Assembly

Sew the blocks together into rows of 4. Press the seam allowances to one side so the rows will nest together. Refer to the photo for color placement. Notice that all the legs of the stars surrounded by light fabric go toward the center of the quilt while the legs surrounded by the medium fabric always point toward the outside corners of the quilt.

It can be quite challenging to make all the points meet since you have 12 seams meeting at the 4 corners. To make it easier to match the points, remove the paper *only* where the points meet. This will cut down on the bulk at the intersections.

Borders

Measure the quilt through the center. It should measure 60 1/2" x 75 1/2". If your quilt doesn't equal this measurement, adjust the length of the borders.

Cut 4 – 5 1/2" x 38" strips from the medium brown border fabric.

1.

Align the Border Trimming Template with the straight edges touching the straight edges of the border. Using your rotary cutter, cut along the angle. Cut 2 strips like this.

2.

To make the remaining 2 strips, invert the Border Trimming Template and align the straight edges with the end and side of each strip and cut the angle.

3.

Trim the 4 reserved light triangles using the Border Triangle Template. Pin each triangle to a border strip and sew along the angle. Press toward the darker fabric.

Sew the strips together for the side borders.

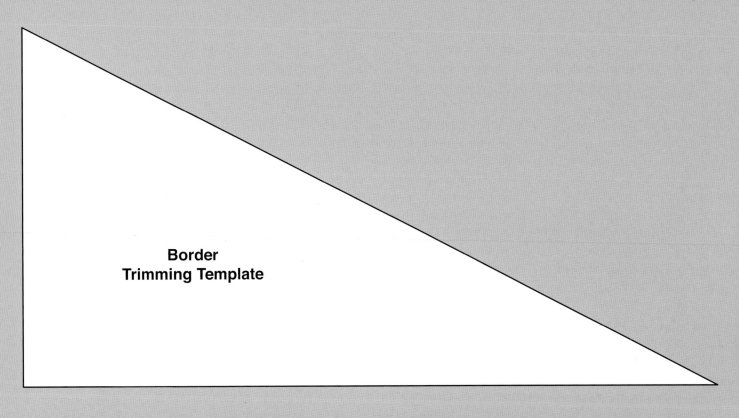

**Border
Trimming Template**

Sew the borders to the quilt. The 2 triangles in the border will align with the 2 on the outer edge of the quilt center and form a diamond shape identical to the ones in the quilt center. Refer to the photo if necessary.

Make 2 border strips 5 1/2" x 60 1/2". Sew a light corner square to each end. Sew one border to the top and one to the bottom of the quilt to finish your top. Remove all the paper then layer the top with batting and backing. Quilt.

Bind the quilt using narrow bias binding. (When I make my binding, I cut bias strips 2" wide, fold in half and stitch to the front of the quilt. I then whipstitch it to the back.)

**Border Triangle Template
Cut 2 & 2 reverse**

Espresso
By Edie McGinnis

Quilted by Lori Kukuk
Quilt size: 41" square
Block sizes: 15" and 5 1/2" finished

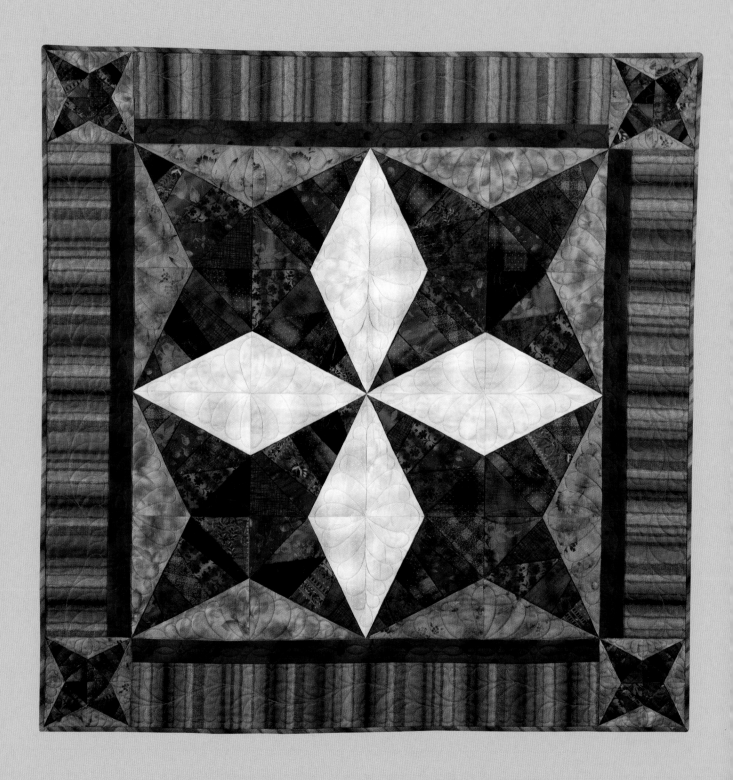

Fabric Requirements

❖   1 fat quarter each of 2 different light blues

❖   1 fat quarter each of 2 different medium tans

❖   1 fat quarter each of 8 different dark browns or assorted fabric to total 1 3/4 yards

❖   1/3 yard of another dark brown (inner border)

❖   1 1/4 yards striped fabric for outside border and binding

Supply List

❖   12" Add-A-Quarter ruler

❖   6" Add-An-Eighth ruler

❖   Foundation Paper – I recommend using Carol Doak's Foundation Paper. You need to make
    4 – 15" blocks and 4 – 5 1/2" blocks. Each large block uses 2 – A units and 2 – B units, so make 8
    copies of each unit.

❖   You need 4 copies of the page with the 5 1/2" pattern.

❖   Rotary cutter

❖   Rotary cutting mat

❖   Double-sided sticky tape

Cutting Directions
15" Blocks

For positions 8 and 9 for both Unit A and Unit B (see pages 14 and 15).

From the 2 light blue fat quarters, cut
4 – 6" x 10" rectangles from each
Place one rectangle atop another with right sides facing. Cut once from corner to corner on the diagonal.

From the 2 medium tan fat quarters, cut
4 – 6" x 10" rectangles from each
Place one rectangle atop another with right sides facing. Cut once from corner to corner on the diagonal.

Note: The objective is to have reverse pieces for positions 8 and 9 on both units. The easiest way to accomplish this is to make sure your fabric is folded with right sides facing before making any cuts.

From the dark brown fat quarters, cut the following pieces. You will want to mix up the browns and sew them into different positions to add interest and contrast to the blocks. Don't hesitate to layer the fabrics to speed up the cutting process.

Unit A – position 3 and Unit B – position 1 – Cut 8 – 5" squares.
Cut the squares once on the diagonal making 16 triangles.

Unit A – position 1	8 – 5 1/4" x 3 1/2" rectangles
Unit A – position 2	8 – 6" x 3" rectangles
Unit A – position 4	8 – 4 1/2" x 3" rectangles
Unit A – position 5	8 – 3 1/2" x 2 1/4" rectangles
Unit A – position 6	8 – 2 1/2" x 2 1/4" rectangles
Unit A – position 7	8 – 1 3/4" x 2 1/2" rectangles
Unit B – position 2	8 – 6 1/4" x 2 1/2" rectangles
Unit B – position 3	8 – 5 3/4" x 3" rectangles
Unit B – position 4	8 – 4 3/4" x 2 3/4" rectangles
Unit B – position 5	8 – 3 3/4" x 3" rectangles
Unit B – position 6	8 – 2 3/4" x 2" rectangles
Unit B – position 7	8 – 1 3/4" x 2 1/2" rectangles

Cutting Directions
5 1/2" Blocks
Use as many of your scraps from the 15" block as you like.

For positions 8 and 9 for both Unit A and Unit B (see pages 14 and 15).

From the 2 medium tan fat quarters, cut
4 – 3" x 4" rectangles from one tan and 4 from the other
Place one rectangle atop another with right sides facing. Cut once from corner to corner on the diagonal.

Note: The objective is to have reverse pieces for positions 8 and 9 on both units. The easiest way to accomplish this is to make sure your fabric is folded with right sides facing before making any cuts.

From the dark brown fat quarters, cut the following pieces. You will want to mix up the browns and sew them into different positions to add interest and contrast to the blocks. Don't hesitate to layer the fabrics to speed up the cutting process.

Unit A - position 3 and Unit B – position 1 – Cut 8 – 2 3/4" squares.
Cut the squares once on the diagonal making 16 triangles.

Unit A – position 1	8 – 2 1/2" x 1 3/4" rectangles
Unit A – position 2	8 – 3" x 2" rectangles
Unit A – position 4	8 – 2 3/4" x 1 3/4" rectangles
Unit A – position 5	8 – 2" x 1 1/2" rectangles
Unit A – position 6	8 – 1 1/2" x 1 1/2" squares
Unit A – position 7	8 – 1 1/2" x 1 1/2" squares
Unit B – position 2	8 – 3" x 1 1/2" rectangles
Unit B – position 3	8 – 2 3/4" x 1 3/4" rectangles
Unit B – position 4	8 – 2 1/2" x 1 3/4" rectangles
Unit B – position 5	8 – 2" x 1 3/4" rectangles
Unit B – position 6	8 – 1 1/2" x 1 1/4" rectangles
Unit B – position 7	8 – 1 1/2" x 1 1/2" squares

Piecing the Units

Refer to Piecing the Units for Café au Lait on page 8. Use the Add-A-Quarter ruler to trim the large blocks and the Add-An-Eighth for the small blocks.

Completing the Units

Trim each of the units before sewing them together. To do so, place the 1/4" line of a rotary cutting ruler on the outside solid line of the pattern. Then trim using your rotary cutter.

Before sewing the 4 sections of the block together, pin at each seam juncture. Baste only where the seams need to meet, using a large stitch on your machine. (Three stitches should do it.) Open and check to make sure the seams are matching, then sew the blocks together using a short stitch. Press as you sew.

1.
Make 4 – 15" blocks. Use light blue fabric around both sides of I leg of the star and medium fabric around both sides of 1 leg of the star. For the 2 remaining legs, use 1 medium and 1 light blue on either side of the legs.

2.
Make 4 – 5 1/2" border blocks using medium fabric around all 4 legs of the star.

Quilt Assembly

Sew the large blocks together. Press the seam allowances to one side so the rows will nest together. Refer to the photo for color placement.

Notice that all the units with the tan in positions 8 and 9 go toward the outside of the quilt and all that use blue in those positions go toward the inside of the quilt.

It can be quite challenging to make all the points meet since you have 12 seams meeting at the 4 corners. To make it easier to match the points, remove the paper *only* where the points meet. This will cut down on the bulk at the intersections.

Borders

Measure the quilt through the center. Cut 4 – 2" strips of the dark brown inner border and trim each to the measured length. Cut 4 – 4 1/2" strips of the striped fabric and trim each to the same length.

Stitch the dark brown inner border strips to the striped border strips. Sew one to either side of the quilt with the dark brown toward the center of the quilt.

Sew a small block to each end of the 2 remaining border strips. Sew these borders to the top and bottom of the quilt to finish your top. Remove all the paper then layer the top with batting and backing. Quilt.

Cut 2" strips on the bias from the remaining striped fabric to make your binding.

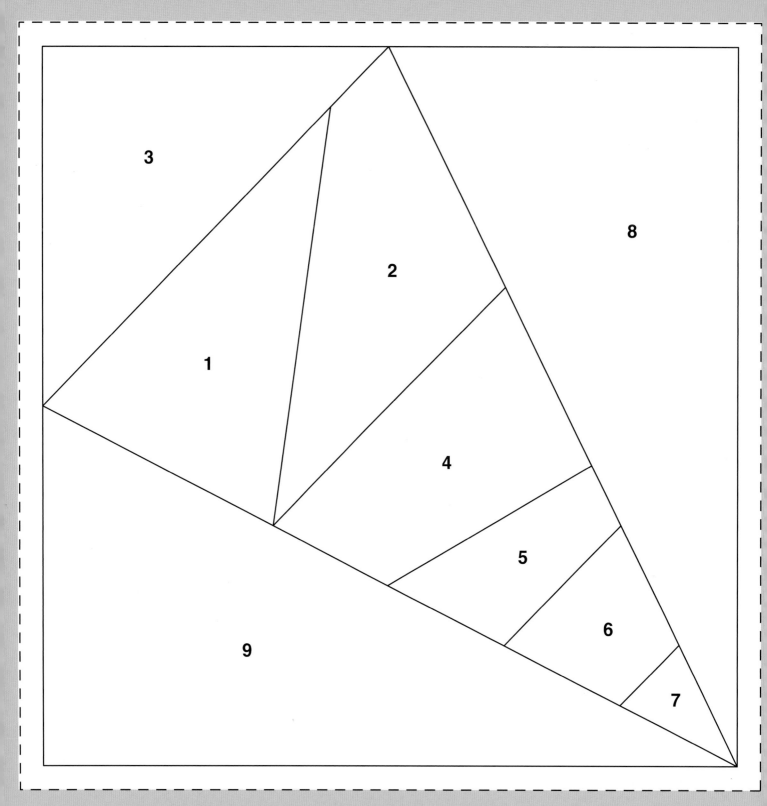

Unit A

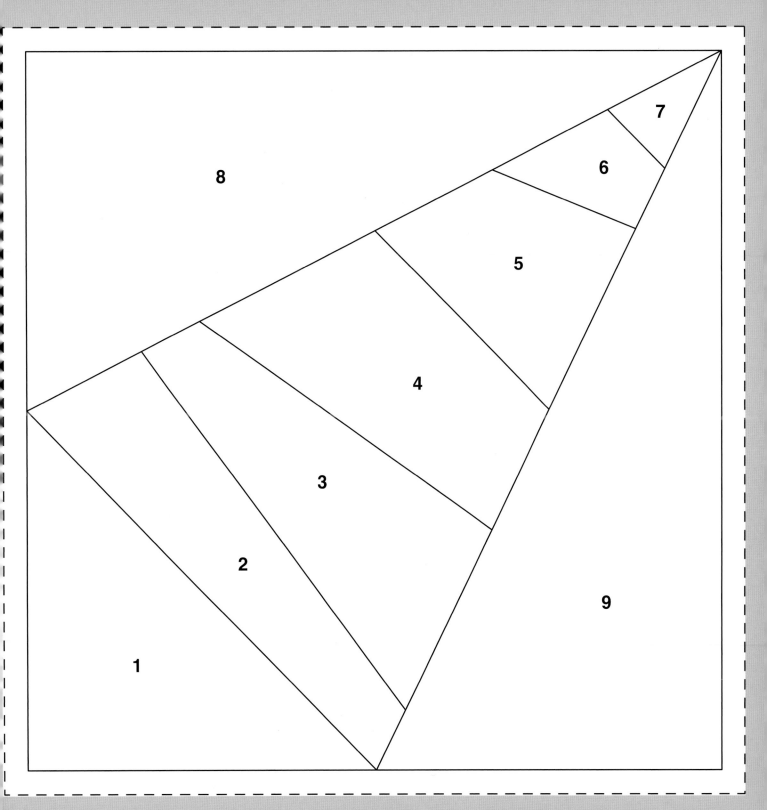

Unit B

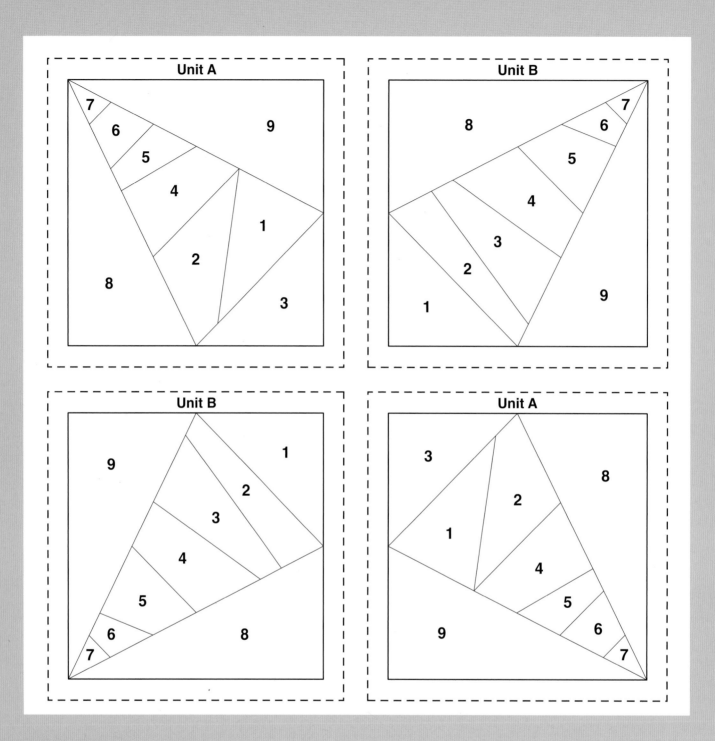